COMPANION PLANTING:

THE ULTIMATE COMPANION GARDENING GUIDE

By Thomas Ribble

Table of Contents

Introduction

Surely by now you have gained interest in companion planting, but at the same time you may be in doubt as to whether or not this thing really works. Well, here are some facts that will likely convince you that companion planting is no joke and that several individuals have actually experienced the marvellous results.

Companion planting promotes the maximum growth and development of the plants placed side by side in a plot. One way it works is based on the amount of shading that is necessary for the promotion of optimal growth. Some plants may require minimal shade while others seem to grow best when not exposed to too much sunlight. Being the case, one plant could actually provide the shade that the other plant needs so that both benefit from this set up.

Some plants produce chemicals or substances and efficiently export them out of the system without harming themselves or the plants surrounding them. What is beneficial about these substances is that they actually promote the growth of neighbouring plants as the chemicals appear to act as signals or sensors, which promote production of substances in the other plant. The substances appear to be advantageous to the plant as they encourage food production or cell propagation.

Some substances produced by the plants also seemed to have a negative impact on many pests. The substances appear to be detrimental or irritating to the animals and so they do not actually land and feed on the plants. A typical example would be onions. When planted together with another plant, onions produce substances that drive pests away. Still others have secretions that tend to redirect the pests or insects away from the more desirable plants to plants that are less palatable to them.

The sweet smelling flower, when planted beside a plant that is typically monochrome, attracts pollinators that can potentially pollinate both plants. As a result, you get your plants propagated faster and enhance genetic quality as self-pollination is less likely to happen.

Advantages of Companion Planting

Companion planting is pretty much a bandwagon these days. In fact, you might find that your neighbors are already creating their own version of a companion garden.

So what's the deal with this form of planting and why should you be enticed to join those who are currently practicing this? You can actually look at these advantages from two angles: what you can directly obtain and what you can contribute for the sustenance and perhaps preservation of the environment.

Direct Benefits

You plant because you perhaps intend to have a fresh source of veggies, herbs, and cut flowers without leaving your home or rummaging through the bins in the supermarket. One of the direct benefits is you can actually harvest healthier and better quality crops. This is because the plants actually help each other to grow not just vigorously but also reach their best potential.

The crops produced from companion planting are also better not just in appearance but in taste. You enjoy more of the produce of your home garden and so you can savor more great recipes, which you can enjoy alone or with the company of your family members and friends.

The old adage "Catching two birds with one stone" actually applies when you practice companion planting. This is because the plants that you beside each other need not be all veggies or all flowers. In fact, most popular combinations are those of vegetables and a flower or herbs and a flower. Therefore, you need not have several plots for a single plot; for instance you may actually have a source of fresh cuts of flowers and healthy veggie choices.

Your home plots will never look as ordinary as before. The mixture of different plants improves the appearance of your garden plots. Unlike the typical monotonous look, your garden will have an eye-catching and enticing transformation. This is possible because you tend to do strip planting, where one strip will be filled with flowers and the parallel strip is planted with a green, leafy veggie.

Companion planting does not require a large patch of land. Even if you have just a small area on your lawn that you can allot for planting, you will harvest a variety of fresh crops. In this way, you do not leave a portion of your lawn idle but instead maximize what you can actually do with just a small space.

What's Companion Planting?

Some individuals may consider companion planting to be some kind of 'New Age' holistic fad; however as the good book says 'There is nothing new under the sun.'

Although the whole aspect of companion planting seems finally to have gathered some recognition; the fact is that it has been practiced for centuries – ever since man first picked up a shovel and decided to grow his own food rather than (or as well as), chase it around with a bow and arrow!

In fact companion planting could be seen as the very foundation stone upon which the whole organic or green movement is built; the reason for this is simple. If done properly, companion planting does away with the need for chemical fertilisers and bug sprays; produces the best, healthy crops; and is the most environmentally friendly way to produce your own fresh food as a consequence.

Not only can you save money by 'going green,' but by making use of the companion planting methods described in this book, you – and your children – can live healthier lives by cutting out the chemical fertilizers and pesticides, that are inevitably included in the daily diet of those individuals who couldn't care less about what they consume, or indeed how it has been grown.

So what is Companion Planting?

Companion planting is simply a form of polyculture, and when used intelligently along with gardening techniques such as Raised Bed Gardening, Square Foot Gardening, or Container Gardening for instance; then this method of sharing the mutual benefits of the individual plants, is capable of producing fantastic results.

In fact, companion planting is likened to putting together the perfect partnership; creating results in respect of larger, healthier crops that the individual plants could not produce.

The fact is that, just like we homo-sapiens; plants need good companions to thrive and flourish in their environment. Unlike us however, being rooted to the spot, they cannot choose their friends – we have to choose friends or companions for them!

How do we choose 'friends' that they will like, and get along with? Simple really. We take into account the strong points and needs of the individual plants, and then put them together – in fact the gardener takes on the role of match-maker!

I'll bet you never considered running a dating agency for vegetables before this – did you? Joking apart; the fact is that if the plants thrive – alongside the ideal companions that you have provided - then the harvest is bountiful – and everyone is happy.

Companion planting is the planting of different plants in close proximity that will provide different benefits for each other. Some plants will thrive when grown together as they will not be competing for light, other plants will thrive together because one plant will attract beneficial insects and the other plant will provide shelter. It is a beneficial relationship between different plants.

Using companion planting to its maximum not only increases the likelihood of thriving plants but it also give you an opportunity to make better use of your available space. Creating this diversity creates an environment that is more similar to growing conditions found in the wild.

Our obsession with planting large groupings of similar plants, often referred to as monoculture has exposed our food crops to a greatly increased risk of attack from disease and insects. Crop rotation can help to reduce the risk but crop rotation alone is not enough.

History of Companion Planting

The history of companion planting is not particularly known as it isn't very well documented. There are stories and oral traditions from cultures all over the world, but the origins are not clear. The three sisters' method of growing corn, squash, and beans is thought to date back thousands of years to when humans first inhabited the Americas. In China, mosquito ferns have been planted with rice crops to fix nitrogen for at least a thousand years.

As the organic culture became more popular in the late 1960's and 1970's, so companion planting also grew in popularity as a natural method of gardening. For many home gardeners, reducing the requirement for chemicals can only be a good thing, and it benefits the environment and wildlife too.

Companion planting is considered a traditional practice when growing fruit and vegetables on a smaller scale, typically used by the backyard gardener or allotmenteer. In the last thirty to forty years though, it has developed as a practice used in larger scale operations, which includes intercropping.

With a strong focus from the scientific community on improving food production while promoting sustainable farming practices, companion planting is gaining ground as scientists conclude what we've been saying for years ... it works!

In more modern times, companion planting became better known in 1943 when Richard B Gregg published a pamphlet entitled "Companion Plants and How to Use Them". Around twenty years later he published a book on the subject which included the results of his own experiments as well as laboratory experiments performed by Dr. Ehrenfried Pfeiffer.

Benefit of Companion Planting

Benefits of Companion Planting

Companion planting is receiving a lot of attention from the scientific community because it can help reduce the need for harmful chemicals in farming. Home gardeners are re-discovering this information and using it to their benefit.

There are several different ways in which companion planting can help you, including:

- Pest Repellent – certain plants give off chemicals either from their leaves, flowers or roots which will repel or suppress pests, protecting its neighbors. Some pests spread diseases, but keeping the bugs under control will help prevent those diseases taking over your plot. A lot of gardeners will use chemicals to control pests, so this natural pest control is more in line with organic gardening methods and helps reduce your need for chemical sprays. Catnip, for example, can repel aphids, ants, and weevils, but also keeps mice away, but not just because it attracts cats. It can take as long as a year or two for natural chemicals to build up in the soil to provide this defense, as is the case with marigolds, which deter nematodes. Some people will claim that companion planting doesn't work purely because they've not given the plants enough time to work their magic.

- Nitrogen Fixers – beans, clover, peas and some other plants have nodules on the roots which grow Rhizobium bacteria. These helpful bacteria take nitrogen from the atmosphere and fix it into the soil in a form that can be used by plants. This nitrogen fixing also benefits neighboring plants as well as later crops planted in the same location.

- Sacrificial Planting – if you have a plant that is particularly susceptible to a pest, you plant another plant nearby that the pests prefer as a decoy. The pests flock to that plant, rather than your vegetable crop. You will still get some pests on your vegetables, but not as many. Most of them will be on the sacrificial plant and can then be easily disposed of. Collard greens planted near cabbage keeps the diamondback moth away as they are more attracted to the greens. Mustard is another trap crop as it attracts cabbage worms (caterpillars) and harlequin bugs, which are extremely destructive to everything from cabbages to radishes for beetroot and potatoes, to mention just a few. Don't pull the mustard up to dispose of the harlequin bugs because they will fall off and make their way to other plants. Dunk the stems (by bending them) into soapy water, so the bugs drown. Plant mustard with clover or dill to attract parasitic wasps, which will prey on the harlequin bugs.

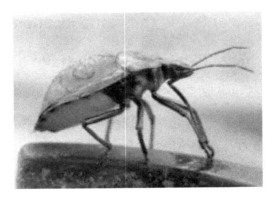

- Enhancing Flavor – some pairings will improve the flavor of your vegetable crop. One of the best-known examples of this is the pairing of basil and tomatoes. These work fantastically in the kitchen, but when grown together, the basil makes the tomatoes more flavorsome. Many herbs, when grown with vegetables, improve their flavor. German chamomile (wild chamomile) improves the flavor and growth of onions, cabbages, and cucumbers.

- Camouflage - a lot of pests use smell to find your precious crops or they look for the shape of your plant. By choosing companion plants with a strong smell, you can confuse many pests. For those pests that hunt by sight, companion plants can confuse the shape of the plant too.

- Shading – known as stacking in permaculture or as level interactions, this is the principle of planting taller plants so that they provide shelter and shade for more delicate plants. This relies on you knowing the path of the sun through the sky. One example of this is the three sisters method of planting where the corn provides welcome shade for the squash plants.

- Attracting Beneficial Insects – your garden needs pollinators as well as pest predators such as hoverflies, lacewings, spiders, parasitic wasps, predatory mites, and ladybirds. Planting the right companion plants will attract insects, which will keep the problem pests down and pollinate your vegetable plants. Creating the right environment for these beneficial insects will encourage them to spend their entire life-cycle in your vegetable garden. This is more important than you may think because it is the larvae of many insects that devour problem pests.

- Increasing Biodiversity – a good mix of plants creates a much more resilient ecosystem. Pests, adverse weather conditions, and diseases will not wipe out your entire crop, but instead just damage a portion of it, and even that can be minimized with the right planting.

Companion planting has a lot of benefits, and it is something that many more gardeners can benefit from. In this book, you will learn how you can use companion planting in your vegetable garden and increase your yields while decreasing your work. It doesn't take up extra space and doesn't detract from your main crops. It means your plants are healthier, grow better and can taste much nicer.

Companion Planting Strategies

For people with limited space, a garden that uses companion planting is the perfect solution to growing vegetable plants and increase their harvest.

In order to make this practice work however, it is necessary to do some planning ahead of time on your part to optimize the yield when harvest time rolls around.

But there are some tips that will definitely increase the output of your crops during this season. They have been found to work very well with the companion planting method and are mutually beneficial to both plant types.

There are many different benefits to this practice and some of the more popular ones include increasing the size and number of produce that is made, repelling garden pests that may otherwise wreak havoc on your plants and attract beneficial predators that can eat the invaders and keep your plot safe.

Just because you have limited space doesn't mean that you can't enjoy a bumper crop of vegetables. By putting some of the following methods to use, you will see some marvelous results in the fall.

One such way is through interplanting. This is slightly different from companion planting in that it makes the most use of a small plot and the plants typically have more than one purpose. A perfect example of this method is using squash and corn in the same area along with bean plants. The corn stalks tend to grow tall and act as a support for the bean vines, while the squash produces large leaves that not only shield the ground to deter weed growth but also act as a natural barrier to corn pests.

Vegetables and flowers can also be interplanted for good results. This is actually one of the best ways to attract pollinators and natural predators to garden pests.

Succession planting is another popular method of putting in a garden plot and this has been used to extend the growing season.

There are actually 4 ways that succession planting can be implemented. The first involves planting the same species but putting plants in at different time intervals. The second entails planting different vegetables in successive periods. You can also plant 2 vegetables in the same area in the third method, while the fourth way is planting the same vegetable but using ones that mature at different rates.

A final option is putting in plants that are annuals (i.e. they only need to be put in once) in order to enjoy multiple yields from one planting. These include such things as asparagus; rhubarb and sweet potatoes just to name a few of the more popular varieties. With the proper soil preparation, you can plant any number of varieties and enjoy a bountiful harvest for many years.

Grow Your Own Companion Herb Garden

The best thing about growing an herb garden is the ease of maintenance. Most of them don't need daily watering or fertilization. But you still need to weed!

Most veteran gardeners use a technique called deep watering which means irrigating the area until there are small puddles evident.

Pest issues are another story altogether. Since you will want to eat these plants at some point, an organic method is preferred to treat them. It's not hard so don't fret about making your own solution. In a one quart hand held sprayer, add a squirt of ivory soap or baby shampoo, then fill with warm water.

NEVER use detergent in this manner. This is just the basic formulas as it can be added to as necessary when combating a specific pest. You should always test the mixture in a small area before proceeding to make sure that the plants are resistant.

If you want to make sure it sticks well to the plants, add 1 teaspoon of vegetable oil. You can also take 1/2 cup of mineral oil and add crushed garlic cloves to it. Strain this mixture after letting it stand for 48 hours. Add about 1 teaspoon to the water/soap mixture.

Another alternative uses one bulb of garlic and an onion. Puree this in a blender/food processor. Put into one cup of olive oil and let sit for 48 hours. Strain the mixture and throw out the pulp. Now add 1/2 teaspoon of cayenne pepper and store in a glass jar. You can add 1 teaspoon to the soap spray as needed.

If you would rather not use any type of spray in your plot, there is always companion gardening. This means planting herbs next to plant to keep bugs away. Just find a plant that has a natural predatory insect such as aphids and plant an herb next to it in order to keep them at bay. This is just one good example of using herbs in order to combat these types of insects naturally, so you may want to do further research on specific companion types.

However, using herb plants as a natural means of keeping out invaders is a great way to still enjoy your garden time and avoid the use of unnecessary chemicals that not only enter the water supply, but become a part of the food chain as well.

Types of Insects: Good and Bad Insects

Good Insects

There are literally millions of types of insect, but not all of them are pests determined to devour your crops. There are a lot of species which are referred to under the umbrella term of 'beneficial insects' which provide a natural form of pest control. For many gardeners, including myself, they are an essential part of organic and natural gardening.

Here are some of the most commonly found beneficial insects with information about what they eat and the environment they prefer.

Ladybugs

These carnivorous insects feed on green and black aphids as well as red spider mites. Organic growers and gardeners love them, trying to attract these into their gardens. Every year ladybugs, or ladybirds as they are known in the UK, will lay hundreds of eggs. The larvae will eat thousands of aphids before maturing, hence the importance of providing a habitat for both this insect in both adult and larvae form. Typically, a ladybug will live for up to three years so long as it avoids being another predators lunch!

There are several plants that attract ladybugs, including:

- Tansy
- Fennel
- Dill
- Cinquefoil
- Yarrow
- Alyssum
- Penstemon

Ladybugs feed on some common garden pests, including:

- Aphids
- Colorado potato beetles
- Fleas
- Mites
- Whitefly

Spiders

A surprising number of people don't like spiders, which is understandable as they aren't my favorite critter either. However, they are very useful in the garden as they eat a lot of different pests. Spiders will naturally find a home in your garden, but you can attract more to your vegetable plot.

Ground Beetles

These are your best friend as they are very voracious predators. These will eat almost anything, but are particularly fond of slugs and snails! Their eating habits will mean they won't get invited to the dinner table; they vomit on their prey, and the digestive enzymes start to dissolve their food.

Ground beetles are often killed by beer traps put down for slugs, as they walk along and fall in. Make sure there is a lip on your beer trap which will prevent these beneficial predators from drowning in the beer.

Most ground beetles are nocturnal and need somewhere shady to hide during the day. A pile of stones or logs or some leaf litter will give them a good place to hide out during the day.

Ground beetles are attracted to your garden by several plants, including:

- Clover

- Amaranthus

- Evening Primrose

The ground beetle will dine on many different pests, including:

- Slugs and snails

- Cutworms

- Colorado potato beetles

- Caterpillars

These are definitely worth protecting and looking after in your garden because they will help to keep the pest levels down naturally.

Parasitic (Braconid) Wasps

These are very different from the wasps that bother a lot of gardeners. They tend to be smaller and will not sting you, unlike their bigger and more vicious cousins.

The lifecycle of these wasps is considered a little gruesome, but they benefit your garden in helping to control pest levels. This wasp will lay its egg in host insects. Once the egg has hatched, the larvae eat the host alive and then emerge as an adult. This family of wasps hunts many different pests including caterpillars, ants, aphids, and sawflies.

A wide variety of plants attracts parasitic wasps, including:

- Yarrow
- Dill
- Parsley
- Lemon Balm
- Lobelia
- Marigold
- Cosmos
- Alyssum

- Cinquefoil

They prey on a lot of different destructive insects, including:

- Aphids

- Caterpillars

- Tomato hornworm

- Tobacco hornworm

Damsel Bugs

Another great insect to attract into your garden, these are not fussy eaters and will prey on pretty much any insect that causes problems in your garden. In Europe, they live in orchards where they eat gypsy moths and red spider mites. This insect will overwinter in vegetation and appreciates somewhere to hide out between meals.

Damsel bugs are attracted to your garden by plants including:

- Alfalfa,

- Fennel

- Caraway

- Spearmint

They eat lots of common garden pests, including:

- Aphids

- Cabbage worms

- Caterpillars

- Corn earworms

- Leafhoppers

- Potato beetles

- Spider mites

By growing some ground cover and low hanging plants, you can attract damsel bugs into your garden where they can help control pests.

Green Lacewings

These are particularly attractive insects that are common in British gardens. With their delicate, lacy wings you could be forgiven for thinking these innocent little creatures are of no use in your garden.

Don't be fooled by their good looks! These are voracious predators in both adult and larvae forms and will eat vast amounts of insect eggs and aphids. The larvae have large jaws which interlock to make pincers on which their prey is impaled. The larvae are very good at clearing your garden of soft-bodied pests.

Lacewings are attracted into your garden by several different plants, including:

- Angelica
- Coriander
- Cosmos
- Dandelion
- Dill
- Fennel

- Yarrow

Some of the insects eaten by lacewings include:

- Aphids

- Caterpillars

- Leafhoppers

- Mealybugs

- Whitefly

Soldier Beetles

Both adults and larvae are useful in pest control. The female lays her eggs in the soil where they overwinter, pupating in the spring. Therefore, you need to leave some areas of soil undisturbed overwinter so these eggs can mature.

Soldier beetles also eat pollen, so pollen-bearing plants can help to attract them into your garden. Other plants that attract them include:

- Goldenrod

- Marigold

- Milkweed

- Wild lettuce

- Zinnia

These beneficial insects prey on many different insects, including:

- Aphids

- Caterpillars

- Corn rootworms

- Cucumber beetles

- Grasshopper eggs

These are an interesting insect to look at and will help keep pests under control.

Tachinid Flies

Adult tachinid flies closely resemble the typical housefly and so are often mistaken for them. These are a parasitic insect and lay its eggs in host insects. Depending on the species of fly, either eggs or live young are placed inside a host insect where they then eat their way out. Some species will even lay eggs on plants where host insects live which then hatch and eat them.

Tachinid flies can be bought, or you can attract them into your garden with a variety of plants including:

- Aster
- Buckwheat
- Carrots
- Cilantro (coriander)
- Chamomile
- Dill
- Fennel
- Feverfew
- Parsley
- Ox-eye and Shasta daisies

They prey on a lot of different pests, including:

- Caterpillars
- Colorado potato beetles
- Corn earworms
- Cutworms
- Earwigs

- Gypsy moths

- Japanese beetles

- Mexican bean beetles

- Sawfly beetles

- Squash bugs

Hoverflies

These are frequently confused with wasps as they share a black and yellow coloring, but they do not sting. They also hover (which wasps do not), do not have long antennae and are typically smaller than stinging wasps. There are lots of different species of hoverfly, and they can fly as fast as 40km/h in short bursts.

Hoverflies will naturally find their way into your garden, but you can attract more of them with plants such as:

- Alyssum

- Cosmos

- Dill

- Lemon balm

- Mallow

- Marigold

- Yarrow

Hoverfly larvae prey on some garden pests including:

- Aphids

- Caterpillars

- Scale insects

Predatory Mites

Humid environments attract these mites such as polytunnels (hoop houses) and greenhouses, where they are most welcome as they prey on spider mites! Spider mites can be a serious problem in greenhouses and very hard to control.

Predatory mites can find their way into your greenhouse, but more often people will buy these beneficial insects and introduce them to the environment.

When there are no spider mites for them to feed on, they will feed on pollen from your plants, helping with pollination.

Solitary Bees

There are lots of species of solitary bee, which does not live in colonies, choosing to live by itself instead. In Britain alone, there are over 200 different species of solitary bee, including the masonry bee, which is often mistaken for a hornet or wasp.

These bees can look like wasps or honeybees, but they are no threat whatsoever to you. The females dig nests, which are then stocked with food (nectar and pollen) and sealed. The young are left to fend for themselves. These bees will usually nest under the ground, often being found under sheds, in piles or logs and so on. You can help encourage them to your garden by making an insect hotel.

These are vital pollinators and should be encouraged into your garden with flowering plants such as:

- Catnip
- Fuchsia
- Heather
- Lavender
- Marjoram

- Viburnum

You now know about some of the beneficial insects that you want to attract into your garden. Of course, there are many more insects, and some will depend on where in the world you live. In some area praying mantis is a beneficial insect, but here in England, I won't ever see one in the wild.

Growing the right types of plants will help attract these insects into your garden and should be part of any gardener's plan. Chemicals should be avoided where possible because they indiscriminately kill both beneficial and harmful insects. With certain chemicals, the residue will persist for the rest of the growing season, which can prevent beneficial insects from returning.

Bad Insects

While the perfect garden would only attract beneficial insects that would prey on anything and everything that dared step foot into the garden, that's rarely the case. Most gardens contain a wide variety of insects, both good and bad.

Let's take a closer look at some of the more common pests found in gardens across the country. If you're lucky, you won't have to deal with more than one or two of these insects at once.

Aphids

Aphids, also known as plant lice, are tiny little insects that can quickly multiply into a huge problem that spans across the vast majority of a garden. A single aphid making its way into an unprotected garden can result in millions or even billions of aphids quickly populating every nook, cranny and corner of your garden.

Aphids can have up to 12 live babies per day. Within the first week, one aphid can have 84 babies. Within a week those aphids are ready to start having babies of their own. The 84 babies will start adding 12 babies apiece per day, which is more than 1,000 aphids being added daily. Once they start having babies, the numbers jump even more dramatically. Within a month, millions of aphids will be infesting the garden. Of course, this simple scenario assumes no aphids die and that each of the aphids has exactly 12 babies per day, but you get the point.

Luckily, you have some options when it comes to controlling aphids. You can plant caraway, chamomile, dandelions, buckwheat and tansy to attract insects that prey on them. Ladybugs, green lacewings, praying mantises and minute pirate bugs will all make a meal of aphids. Nasturtiums can be used as a trap crop for aphids.

Additionally, you can use the following plants to repel aphids

- Basil.
- Catnip.
- Chives.
- Clover.
- Coriander.
- Dill.
- Eucalyptus.
- Fennel.
- Garlic.
- Onions.
- Nettles.
- Peppermint.
- Radishes.

A combination of plants that attract insects that attack aphids and plants that aphids don't care for seems to be the best way to prevent aphids from making their way into the garden. If you catch an infestation while it's underway, use a strong spray of water to wash aphids away from your plants. Watch your plants closely after that and wash them down again if the aphids return.

Asparagus Beetles

Asparagus beetles are orange and white or blue-black beetles that prey on asparagus shoots. From larvae to mature adults, asparagus beetles will make a meal of both the leaves and the stems of the asparagus plant. Knock the larger beetles into a bucket of soap to get rid of them.

Ladybug larvae will eat both the eggs and the larvae of the asparagus beetle, so keep plants that attract ladybugs in your garden. Additionally, the following plants are known to deter asparagus beetles

- Basil.

- Coriander.

- Parsley.

- Petunias.

- Tomatoes.

Cabbage worms and Cabbage Loopers

Cabbage worms and cabbage loopers attack Brassica crops all across North America. They look like white or green caterpillars and will tunnel through the roots of cabbages.

Beneficial nematodes are the main predator needed in the garden to clear out cabbage worms. Nematodes will likely have to be purchased because they're difficult to attract. In addition to adding nematodes to the soil, the following plants can be grown to prevent cabbage worms from ever making their way into a garden:

- Borage.

- Celery.

- Dill.

- Radishes.

- Rosemary.

- Sage.

- Thyme.

- Tomatoes.

Another option is to plant a crop like mustard that attracts cabbage loopers and cabbage worms around the outside of your garden as a trap crop that can be sacrificed to protect more desirable crops.

Caterpillars

Caterpillars attack a wide range of plants, chewing on leaves, tunneling through fruit and leaving droppings behind everywhere they go. While the butterflies some of them will eventually become may be beneficial to a garden, they're quite the pest while in the caterpillar stage. Of particular concern are cutworms and cabbage loopers, which have been known to quickly strip plants of their foliage.

In order to keep caterpillars at bay, add plants to your garden that draw in parasitic wasps, praying mantises and green lacewings. Another option is to hang a bird feeder to call in birds that'll come for the bird food and supplement their meals with any caterpillars that cross their paths. When you see a caterpillar, handpick it and move it far from your garden.

The following plants can be planted in a garden to repel caterpillars:

- Lavender.

- Peppermint.

- Sage.

Colorado potato beetle

The Colorado potato beetle looks like a yellowish-orange ladybug with stripes instead of dots. While ladybugs are a preferred predator in the garden and will eat Colorado potato beetles, these pests will quickly defoliate peppers, potatoes, eggplant and tomatoes. In addition to ladybugs, nematodes are beneficial to have around when potato beetles are present.

Some sources indicate the Colorado potato beetle doesn't like to walk over coarse mulch. Adding a layer of straw mulch around your plants may prevent the beetle from making it to your plants.

The following plants will repel Colorado potato beetles:

- Catnip.

- Chives.

- Coriander.

- Eucalyptus.

- Garlic.

- Green beans.

- Marigolds.

- Nasturtiums.

- Peas.

Flea Beetles

These tiny little pests are found across the entirety of North America. They chew small, round holes in the leaves of most vegetables and will jump around nervously when disturbed. Flea beetles prefer dry soil to lay their eggs in, so keep your soil damp to make your garden less attractive. Nematodes can be added to the soil to make short work of any larvae that do hatch.

The following plants will repel flea beetles:

- Catnip.

- Peppermint.

- Rue.

- Thyme.

Mealybugs

Mealybugs are tiny creatures that appear in clusters at the base of leaves. They'll attack a wide variety of fruit and vegetables, including citrus trees, grapes and potatoes. They suck sap out of plants and leave a honeydew residue behind that can quickly start to mold.

Lacewings and mealybug destroyers enjoy eating mealybugs, so do what it takes to attract them to your garden. Companion planting isn't an effective means of eliminating mealybugs.

Mexican bean beetle

The Mexican bean beetle is a connoisseur of a number of varieties of beans. It has a bottomless pit for a stomach and will continue chewing on the leaves of a plant until it starts to die. These beetles roam the Western half of the United States, looking for bean crops to devastate.

The following plants are known to repel Mexican bean beetles

- Garlic.

- Marigolds.
- Rosemary.

Japanese Beetles

Japanese beetles are commonly found in the Eastern half of the United States and are known to attack a variety of vegetables and flowers. They're a bluish-green color and feature rust-colored wing covers. They're pretty to look at, but the damage they can do to a crop is anything but pretty.

The following plants will deter Japanese beetles:

- Catnip.
- Chives.
- Chrysanthemums.
- Garlic.
- Marigolds.
- Onions.
- Rue.

Scales

Scales are aptly named because, at a glance, they look like small scales attached to a plant. They're destructive little creatures that will suck sap from plants during every stage of their life cycle. When you notice scales on your plants, prune them back to get rid of the affected areas or scrub them off the branches.

There are no plants that are known to deter scales, so you'll have to rely on predatory insects to get the job done. Ladybugs, praying mantises and green lacewings will all dine on scales, so plants that attract them may help.

Thrips

These tiny insects are so small you probably won't see them on your plants. What you will see are discolored areas that take on an almost silvery sheen as the thrips bite into the plants repeatedly and leave a large number of tiny little scars. Thrips aren't problematic unless the population gets out of control and begins to spread viruses. P

Tomato Fruitworms (Corn Earworms)

Tomato fruitworms, also known as corn earworms, cotton bollworms and geranium budworms, are found in gardens throughout North America. These worms are known by a number of names, usually indicative of the type of plant they're attacking. They've been known to dine on cotton, beans, peas, peppers, tomatoes, corn, geraniums, potatoes and squash.

The adults are small moths that lay eggs on the bottoms of leaves. The larvae feed on the leaves as they grow. If they're attacking a corn crop, they'll move into the husks as the corn matures and will eventually begin to feed on the silk and the corn kernels at the ends of the ears.

Geraniums and thyme are known to deter the tomato fruitworm.

Tomato Hornworm

This large caterpillar is found in gardens throughout the United States, usually munching on the leaves of eggplant, peppers, potatoes and tomatoes. They develop into large moths that have a wingspan of up to 5".

The following plants will repel tomato hornworms:

- Borage.

- Dill.

- Thyme.

Garden Planning

The key to successful companion planting is properly planning where the plants in your garden are going to go. You've got to carefully consider how each of the plants in your garden are going to interact with one another and then place them in the best possible locations to take advantage of those interactions. The biggest limitation in regard to companion planting is the knowledge of the gardener. Arm yourself with as much knowledge as possible before you ever put on your gardening gloves.

The first step to proper garden planning is deciding which plants you want in your garden. Create a master list of the plants you absolutely need to have and plan your garden around that list. Once you have a list of essential plants, supplement the list with a handful of other plants you wouldn't mind having.

Now, get to work researching the potential interactions between the plants you need and the plants you'd like to have. Consider allelopathy, pests, beneficial insects, the heights of the plants and the depths of the root systems to create groupings of plants that will work hand-in-hand. Plants that are beneficial to one another should be kept together, while plants that are detrimental to each other should be planted at opposite ends of the garden.

Once you've got your garden planned, take a closer look at the plants you've included in the plans and see if there are any other plants you didn't include that can help. Flowers, ground cover and other smaller good neighbors may be able to be squeezed into small areas of the garden to good effect. With companion planting, you aren't going to have your typical garden with row after orderly row of produce. Instead, you're going have plants that are mixed and matched because of what they can do for one another.

Don't start planting until you've got your garden mapped out. It's the best way to ensure you keep good neighbors together and bad neighbors far apart.

Alfalfa

Alfalfa is primarily grown as a forage crop because it's easy to grow and is a high-value feed crop that's high in protein. It prefers deep, well-drained soil, but can be grown in a wide variety of soil types. Alfalfa sprouts can be consumed by humans, but the full-grown plants are generally used for animal feed.

As far as the home garden is concerned, alfalfa is generally planted as a cover crop that can be grown between crops that place a heavy load on the soil. Plant your garden with alfalfa and turn it into the soil and you'll ensure successive gardens have the nutrients they need to successfully grow.

If you've got hard pan or thick clay soil, alfalfa can be used to break up the soil. It has a deep rooting system and has even been known to push roots through rocks. Avoid planting alfalfa around tomatoes because it has been shown to be allelopathic toward tomato seedlings.

Known Benefits:

Alfalfa increases the level of iron, magnesium, nitrogen, phosphorous and potassium in the soil. It can also be planted to increase the amount of green foliage in the garden in order to confuse pests looking to land on something green. Additionally, alfalfa crops can be planted to provide habitat for predatory and parasitic insects that will prey on pests.

Almonds

If you live in a climate warm enough to grow almonds, consider yourself very lucky. It can take up to 5 years for young trees to start producing, but once they do you'll be able to harvest almonds from them annually for up to 50 years. A single healthy, full-grown tree can produce upwards of 40 pounds of almonds per year.

Almond trees are good to plant around blackberries because they hold moisture in their canopies and drop leaves that turn into mulch.

Known Benefits:

Almonds can hold moisture in their leaves. When the leaves fall they turn into natural organic mulch.

Anise

Anise is a strong-scented herb that has the flavor of licorice. It grows tall, so it can be used to provide shade for low-growing plants. It's said to improve the vigor of any plant grown in close proximity and is a popular choice for flower beds.

Coriander especially benefits from being grown near anise because it speeds up germination. Broccoli and other Brassica family plants benefit from anise because it masks their smell, preventing pests that target their scents.

Known Benefits:

Anise is known to deter lice and some biting insects, while attracting predatory wasps that prey on aphids. The strong scent of anise masks the scent of nearby plants, hiding them from pests.

Apples

Apple trees are a great addition to most backyards. They run the gamut from huge trees that reach more than 25' in height to smaller dwarf or hedge varieties that only grow to 8' to 10' tall, so there's an apple tree for almost any yard. Apple trees can be grown in containers, so you may even be able to grow apples if all you have is a concrete patio.

Apricots

Many apricot varieties are early bloomers and may not be a good choice for areas that get late frosts because a good frost can kill the bloom. When choosing a variety, carefully consider whether you want an early-, midseason- or late-blooming tree.

Apricot trees can reach 30' in height and a single tree can produce up to 100 pounds of apricots. Apricot trees can live up to 70 years.

Asparagus

Asparagus is a dinner-time favorite that tastes equally great whether lightly oiled and tossed on the grill, boiled or steamed. Asparagus stalks can grow to heights of 5' or more, but are rarely allowed to do so because they become woody and inedible. Harvest asparagus for eating when it's around 8" to 10" in height.

This hardy plant is good neighbors with a number of plants and gets along well with most neighbors. When paired with basil, it's believed to draw in ladybugs that keep aphids out of the garden. Comfrey is a good choice because it dies back as the asparagus starts to grow and will provide food for the growing asparagus plants. Just be aware that comfrey can grow out of control and may need to be cut back in order to give asparagus space.

Known Benefits:

Asparagus can be planted around low-growing plants and will provide mottled shade for the plants during the heat of the day. Planting asparagus near tomato plants will help repel the nematodes that attack tomatoes.

Asters

This brightly-colored flower blooms well into the late summer and fall and can add color to a garden long after most summer blooms have lost their luster. Asters range from small in stature at 6" to 8" to very tall, with some varieties reaching heights approaching 8'.

While asters are compatible with most vegetables, they need to be kept away from celery and corn because they're carriers of aster yellows disease, which can cause deformities in the flowers of the aster plant. Asparagus thrives when planted near asters because they repel harmful nematodes and a handful of other insects.

Known Benefits:

Attracts pollinating insects and ladybugs, while repelling nematodes and other insects.

Basil

Basil is a bushy annual garden herb that can grow up to 2' tall. It's a highly fragrant plant used in a wide variety of dishes as a seasoning herb.

Basil is beneficial when planted near most garden crops, as it aids with growth and repels a number of insects. When paired with asparagus, basil is thought to draw ladybugs into the garden. When planted in close proximity to tomatoes, both plants end up tasting better.

Known Benefits:

Basil helps deter fungal growth and is capable of driving away a number of insects, including aphids, asparagus beetles, mites and mosquitoes. In addition to driving away bad insects, basil also attracts butterflies, which can aid with pollination.

Bay

Bay leaves come from the bay laurel tree, which is an evergreen tree native to Greece. It prefers a moderate climate and doesn't do well in areas that experience deep freezes. Bay can be grown in containers, so that may be an option for those looking to grow bay in a cooler climate.

Known Benefits:

Bay leaves will deter weevils and moths. This effect is more pronounced when bay leaves are dried and crushed and dispersed into the soil.

Companion Planting Chart

Sowing, Planting Dates and Temperature Chart

Remember that you will have to use this guide to fit in with the temperature and weather conditions in your local area. Even within one small area there can be variations due to prevailing winds, hills, valleys etc. Your seed packets will provide you with general guidelines buy you will need to consult an experienced local grower for more exact information.

The most important information they can give you will relate to local frost times. This is the key piece of information for using this chart. This is because the sowing dates and planting out dates are based on the approximate date of the last frost in your locality.

Peppers/Chili

Sow 8 weeks prior to last frost date.

Germination temperature needed is 80-85°F

Germination occurs within 10-21 days

Plant out 2 weeks after last frost date.

Tomatoes

Sow 6 weeks prior to last frost date

Germination temperature needed is 75 - 80°F

Germination occurs in 7 – 10 days

Plant out 2 weeks after last frost date.

Broccoli

Sow 8 weeks prior to last frost date

Germination temperature needed is 70 - 75°F

Germination occurs in 7 – 10 days

Plant out 3 weeks before last frost date.

Cabbage

Sow 8 weeks before last frost date

Germination temperature needed is 70 - 75°F

Germination occurs in 6 – 9 days

Plant out 3 weeks before last frost date.

Cauliflower

Sow 7 weeks before last frost date

Germination temperature needed is 70 - 75°F

Germination occurs in 5 – 10 days

Plant out 3 weeks before last frost date.

Kale

Sow 8 weeks before last frost date

Germination temperature needed is 70 - 75°F

Germination occurs in 6 – 9 days

Plant out 3 weeks before last frost date

Eggplant

Sow 8 weeks before last frost date

Germination temperature needed is 80 - 90°F

Germination occurs in 10 – 14 days

Plant out 2 weeks after last frost date.

Leek

Sow 10 weeks before last frost date

Germination temperature needed is 75 - 85°F

Germination occurs in 5 – 10 days

Plant out 2 weeks before last frost date.

Lettuce

Sow 8 weeks prior to last frost date

Germination temperature needed is 65 - 75°F

Germination occurs in 3 – 5 days

Plant out 4 weeks before last frost date

Onion

Sow 10 weeks before last frost date

Germination temperature needed is 70 – 75°F

Germination occurs in 7 – 9 days

Plant out 2 weeks before last frost date

Basil

Sow 3 weeks before last frost date

Germination temperature needed is 70 - 80°F

Germination occurs in 5 -7 days

Plant out 2 weeks after last frost date

Marjoram/Oregano

Sow 6 weeks before last frost date

Germination temperature needed is 65 -75°F

Germination occurs in 7 – 10 days

Plant out 2 weeks after last frost date.

Parsley

Sow 10 weeks before last frost date

Germination temperature needed is 70°F

Germination occurs in 10 – 14 days

Plant out 2 weeks before last frost date.

Canterbury Bells

Sow seeds 5 to 7 weeks prior to last frost date

Germination temperature needed is 60 - 70°F

Germination occurs in 10 – 20 days

Plant out 2 weeks after last frost date.

Carnations

Sow seeds 9 – 10 weeks prior to last frost date

Germination temperature needed is 65 - 75°F

Germination occurs in 10 -20 days

Plant out 2 weeks before last frost date

Columbines

Sow seeds 2 – 5 weeks prior to last frost date

Germination temperature needed is 70 - 75°F

Germination occurs in 20 25 days

Plant out 6 weeks after last frost date

Delphiniums

Sow 2 – 5 weeks prior to last frost date

Germination temperature needed is 65 - 75°F

Germination occurs in 10 – 20 days

Plant out 4 – 7 weeks after last frost date.

Foxglove

Sow seeds 10 – 12 weeks prior to last frost date

Germination temperature needed is 65 -70°F

Germination occurs within 14 -21 days

Plant out 2 weeks before last frost date.

Lobelia

Sow seeds 6 weeks prior to last frost date

Germination temperature needed is 65 - 70°F

Germination occurs in 10 – 14 days

Plant out 2 weeks after last frost date.

Marigolds

Sow seeds 6 – 7 weeks prior to last frost date

Germination temperature needed is 75 - 80°F

Germination occurs in 5 – 7 days

Plant out 2 weeks after last frost date.

Nicotiana

Sow seeds 6 -7 weeks prior to last frost date

Germination temperature needed is 70 -75°F

Germination occurs in 14 – 21 days

Plant out 2 weeks after last frost date

Viola/Pansy

Sow seeds 10 – 12 weeks prior to last frost date

Germination temperature needed is 65 - 70°F

Germination occurs in 10 -14 days

Plant out 2 weeks before last frost date

Petunia

Sow seeds 10 -12 weeks prior to last frost date

Germination temperature needed is 75 -80°F

Germination occurs in 10 -14 days

Plant out 2 weeks after last frost date.

Phlox

Sow seeds 4 weeks prior to last frost date

Germination temperature needed is 60 - 65°F

Germination occurs in 9 – 15 days

Plant out 2 weeks after last frost date.

Snapdragons

Sow seeds 10 – 12 weeks before last frost date

Germination temperature needed is 65 – 70°F

Germination occurs in 7 14 days

Plant out 2 weeks before last frost date.

Statice

Sow seeds 6 – 7 weeks prior to last frost date

Germination temperature needed is 70 -75°F

Germination occurs in 7 – 14 days

Plant out 2 weeks after last frost date.

Stock

Sow seeds 6 – 7 weeks prior to last frost date

Germination temperature needed is 65 - 70°F

Germination occurs in 7 – 10 days

Plant out 2 weeks before last frost date.

Quick Reference Companion Planting Chart:

VEGGIES	GOOD COMPANION	BAD COMPANION
Asparagus	tomato, parsley, basil	onions, garlic, potatoes
Beans	beetroot, cabbage, celery, carrot, cucumber, corn, squash, pea's, potatoes, radish, strawberry.	garlic, shallot or onions

Beets	broccoli, brussels sprouts, bush beans, cabbage, cauliflower	charlock, field mustard, pole beans
Cabbage	cucumber, potato, onion, spinach, celery.	Strawberries
Carrots	beans, peas, onions, leeks, lettuce, tomato, and radish	Dill
Celery	bean, tomato and cabbage family	corn, Irish potato and aster flowers
Corn	potato, pumpkin, squash, tomato, cucumber	Tomatoes
Cucumber	cabbage, beans, radish, tomato	late potatoes
Eggplant	beans, peas, spinach, tarragon, thyme	
Garlic	cabbage, cane fruits, fruit trees, tomatoes	peas, beans

Leeks	Carrots, celery, onions	Legumes
Lettuce	carrot, beet, onion, and strawberry	cabbage family
Melon	pumpkin, radish, corn, and squash	
Onions	cabbage family, beet, tomato, pepper, strawberry, and chard	beans, peas
Parsley	asparagus, carrot, tomato and corn	Mint
Peas	beans, carrot, corn and radish	garlic leeks, onions, shallots
Peppers	tomato, eggplant, carrot and onion	fennel, kohlrabi
Potatoes	bean, cabbage, squash and peas	apples, cherries, cucumbers, pumpkins, sunflowers, tomatoes

Pumpkin	melon eggplant and corn	potato, raspberry
Radish	carrot, cucumber, bean, pea, melon	hyssop
Squash	melon, pumpkin, beans, cucumber, onion	potato, tomato
Strawberry	bean, lettuce, onion and spinach	cabbage, broccoli, Brussels sprouts
Tomatoes	celery, cucumber, asparagus, parsley, pepper and carrot	fennel, kohlrabi, potatoes

Beneficial Herbs

There are many herbs that can be extremely beneficial for your companion planting. Indeed the herbs themselves can lend that extra dimension to your vegetable garden, that will complement your vegetables – and improve your cooking!

Here is a list of some popular herbs along with the benefits they may have to certain plants.

Anise:

Anise is known to benefit beans and coriander plants.

Basil:

This is known to benefit asparagus, beans, cabbage and especially tomatoes.

It can be beneficial also as a 'sacrificial' plant in that it's soft leaves tend to attract butterflies and boring insects.

Caraway:

This is an ideal herb for breaking down and conditioning poor soils. It also attracts the attention of wasps and other harmful insects, making it a good 'sacrificial' herb. Also known to benefit strawberries and peas.

Chives:

An ideal companion for carrots, as it confuses the carrot fly. Also good around peppers, potato, rhubarb, squash or tomato plants, as it deters insects – particularly aphids.

Fennel:

This makes a poor companion plant for just about anything – avoid planting near other plants.

Lavender:

A good companion plant for many species as it's aromatic flowers attract many beneficial, pollinating insects to the garden.

It will also deter fleas, ticks and even mice!

Mint:

This is another all-round beneficial companion for many plant species; and in particular, peas, cabbage and tomatoes.

Mint is known also to deter insects, and even mice from your plants.

Parsley:

Asparagus is known to benefit particularly well, when grown alongside parsley; but carrots, cor, sweet peppers are also good companions.

Avoid planting near mint or lettuce.

Peppermint:

A good companion as it attracts beneficial insects and repels ants, aphids and cabbage fly.

Ways to Feed Your Garden

There are many options available to feed your garden. Some require commercial fertilizers, but the best are ones that you can use without adding chemicals to the soil. These include:

• Monoculture

• Rotation

• Mulches

• Compost

• Garden teas

• Fertilizers

Monoculture

Monoculturing is the process of planting just one type of plant. In companion planting, this practice is used to enrich the soil through the benefits one plant can give. This monoculture plant is then turned back into the soil to increase the nutrient level of the soil. One example of this is to grow alfalfa or another grass crop and turn it back under before it goes to seed to let it decompose further before planting that area of your garden. By doing this, the soil has a chance to rest and replenish itself.

Rotation

Crop rotation is a great way to control insects, weeds, and diseases, and it also enhances soil fertility. Vegetables in the same botanical family will require similar nutrients in similar amounts. Some will be considered heavy feeders like broccoli, sweet corn, and tomatoes, and will utilize more of the soil's nutrients, whereas others are considered light feeders, like carrots, onions, peppers, and potatoes, and will use fewer nutrients. To go along with these plant types, there are plants that add nutrients and improve the soil, like peas and beans. If you practice crop rotation by alternating these three types of crops in one bed, the soil can be enhanced.

Mulches

Mulch is a protective layer placed over the soil. There are many benefits to using mulch including:

• Minimizes weeds — the mulch will suffocate weeds and stop light from reaching the seeds, which stops new weeds from germinating.

• Improves the garden plants — the mulch covers the plant's roots that are on the surface, saving them from damage caused by cultivation and drying out.

• Retains moisture — mulch reduces the amount of evaporation, which keeps the soil moist, and allows for a more even growth.

• Minimizes temperature differences — the mulch minimizes the temperature extremes at the soil level so it stays warmer at night and cooler in the day.

• Improves the soil — if you are using organic mulch, it will add nutrients to the soil as it decomposes, encouraging microbial growth. It also encourages earthworms to burrow in the soil, which aerates and drains the soil. The mulch also prevents the soil from packing down.

• Creates a more even-looking garden — mulch stops the dirt from splashing up onto the plants during rain or watering and from washing the soil away from the plants during too heavy rain or watering.

• Gives the garden a finished look — the garden looks professional with a nice mulch covering it. A uniform layer of good looking mulch throughout the garden gives the area a uniform, "finished" look.

The following are some forms of mulch you may want to consider.

Organic Mulch

There are many types of organic mulch to choose from. There are some you may have readily available and others you may need to buy. Most will be available through your local garden center.

The best organic mulches include:

• Bark or small wood chips — these come as small or large chips (or chip your own if you have a wood chipper) and work well under trees and shrubs. You can purchase finely shredded cedar mulch in various colors that can add an interesting designer component.

• Leaves — fall leaves are great for mulching large open areas, particularly around squash, pumpkin patches, or other sprawling areas. If you are short on another type of mulch, like compost or newspaper, leaves make a great second layer. Not only does it cover up something unsightly, but it also helps with decomposition.

• Eucalyptus — this mulch has to be purchased from your local garden center and comes shredded or as fiber mulch. The advantage of this type of mulch is that the oil in the eucalyptus repels termites, fleas, ticks, and insects. The disadvantage is that it can be hard to obtain and it can be twice as expensive as other types of mulch.

• Grass clippings — when they are fresh, they are smelly and will stain your hands but are high in moisture and nitrogen, making them good for the garden. Avoid using clippings that are full of grass seeds because these seeds are likely to sprout in your garden. This mulch is easy to work with and can be placed throughout the garden where the seedlings are more delicate or closely planted, such as around lettuce, spinach, and carrots.

• Straw — if you have access to straw, it offers excellent winter protection for your garden. The only problem with using straw is the potential for some of the seeds to germinate. Straw should be seed free but because it is often confused with hay, which still has seeds, it is possible to end up with seeds in your bales. Another disadvantage is that it is not very attractive and looks worse as time goes on.

• Pine needles — this is a long-lasting mulch that can slightly acidify the soil under it. This makes it good for potatoes and strawberries, which benefit from the more acidic soil. It is also an easy mulch to put into small or hard-to-reach places. Pine cones can also be used and make an attractive addition to any woodland garden.

• Pine bark — this is a mulch that decomposes slower than other varieties and will last a year or more. It comes in different sizes, ranging from fine to 2-inch chunks. The disadvantage of this mulch is that it can lower the pH slightly. You can still use it around the same plants that prefer a more acidic environment like strawberries.

Non-Organic Mulch

There are several non-organic mulches available on the market. These types of mulches keep the weeds down and do not need replacing like organic mulches. Some of these mulches include:

• Plastic sheeting — these are large sheets of dark plastic. They are great to use in the spring to warm up beds and are also great for suppressing weeds. If you use a heavy grade plastic, which will last many years, you can lay it down between rows of plants where you want more heat, like between tomatoes, or on paths where you want to suppress weeds. You can use the sheeting to help improve the soil by stuffing the underside of the black plastic with organic matter to compost underneath the sheet. Some gardeners even lay the plastic down and cut holes into it to transplant seedlings. The plastic can stay on throughout the whole season as a weed suppressor. The problem with doing this is that it will not let water through it.

• Landscape fabric — this is a loosely woven fabric that helps retain moisture and slows or even prevents weed growth. The disadvantage of this type of mulch is it is usually one of two layers with a top layer covering the fabric to make the garden bed look better. Also consider that some landscape cloths are nonporous and will not let moisture through. If you purchase the nonporous type, the plant roots can suffocate and rot.

• Rubber — this product is made from recycled tires and will not decompose, making it permanent mulch. It can be purchased as mats, tiles, and nuggets and is available in various colors. It will not blow away or wash away under a heavy watering. It also comes in many attractive colors, giving it a strong design element. In practical terms, insects avoid the rubber and it does not sink into the ground like gravel and rocks. However, the product can give off a strong odor and can be both expensive and hard to find.

• Stone (pebbles and gravel) — stones can be as small as pea gravel or as large as small boulders. The small gravel will stop the weeds better, but when topped with an assortment of boulders, together they create a nice contrast for the garden. Stones are another permanent cover as they do not break down over time but offer great color and texture to a garden. The disadvantage is that some of the smaller rocks will disappear into the soil over time and working with this type of mulch is physically demanding.

When to mulch

Lay the mulch down in the garden after the soil has warmed up in the late spring or the early summer. Placing an even, shallow layer of mulch approximately 2 to 4 inches deep will be effective against wind, sun, weeds, and pests. Be careful of the plants and avoid putting the mulch close to the crown of the perennials and the stems or trunks of shrubs and trees as you do not want to damage new growth and you need to leave plants space to obtain water.

If you live in a winter climate, one of the best times to mulch is in winter. Depending on where you live, the freezing and thawing process causes the soil to expand and contract. This can break new roots and even force your plants out of the ground in a process called frost heaves. If you cover the garden with something loose and full of air, like straw, when the ground first freezes, you can help keep the ground frozen until winter ends. Once spring arrives, you can remove the mulch.

Another benefit of winter mulching is protecting all types of plants, including perennials and ground covers, from winter burn, which can happen when the winter temperatures damage the plants. When the ground freezes and there is a strong wind, the moisture is pulled from the plant.

Compost

Compost can be the best natural fertilizer for your garden, regardless of the type of plants you are growing. It is a mixture of decomposed plant and animal material (manure) and many other organic materials that then go through decomposition in the presence of oxygen, called aerobic decomposition, to create a rich black soil. This soil is excellent for your garden as a soil conditioner and fertilizer.

The best compost materials include fruit and vegetable material, garden trimmings (not weeds gone to seed), and animal manure from horses, goats, sheep, and chicken. Other materials to consider adding if you have them available include leaves, coffee grounds, paper, cardboard, seafood shells, tree bark, eggshells, and even "humanure" (human waste).

How to make compost

Choose a spot close enough to be easily accessible but out of sight. You can choose to purchase a compost bin or alternatively build a system to work in the space you have available. You can make a heap in one corner of the garden and use the area to make your compost pile; you can use a single bin and place all the organic material into it; or you can create a three-bin system (made from wood). If you leave the bins open on one side, you can easily add to the pile, and to turn it over occasionally. Only cover the tops of the compost bins if your area receives a lot of rain. The three-bin system allows you to turn the compost from one bin to the other so that the compost in the final bin is ready to use while the pile in the second bin is in the middle stage and the first bin is just starting to decompose. However, you will need to manually move the compost from one bin to the other.

When starting a new compost pile, making a pile with two parts of brown materials to one part green will help the materials break down faster. The green garden materials are grass clipping or old annual plants pulled from the garden, and the brown garden materials are dry leaves and twigs. The green material is high in nitrogen and the brown material is high in carbon and both are required to make your compost work successfully. If you add in too much green, the compost will have a foul odor.

Pile or layer the green and browns into a heap until you have a compost heap that is about 3 feet by 3 feet by 3 feet. You want the pile close to this size because it will heat up quickly and will therefore break down faster. Once a week, check the moisture content of the pile. To decompose properly, your pile will need water, but if there is too much moisture, the pile will not be able to maintain the required heat level. Your compost should feel damp like a wrung out sponge; any more water content than this and the pile will start to smell worse than normal. If your pile is too wet, you can add more leaves; if it is too dry, you can water it gently with a garden hose.

Once a week, the pile needs to be turned over, meaning you turn the outside material into the center – where there is internal compost heat. Oxygen is required for the decomposition process, which is why you turn the pile. Turning the pile also stops it from becoming hard and compacted. Some people keep a perforated PVC pipe standing upright in the center of the compost pile to let oxygen reach the center of the pile.

If you turn your pile over once a week, you could have finished compost in eight to ten weeks. The compost pile that is not turned over will not be as active and will take longer to decompose with the good compost sitting at the bottom of the pile. During the decomposition process, the temperature of the pile will reach between 110 and 160 degrees F. You can monitor the temperature with a long probe thermometer pushed into the center of the pile. Turn the pile when the temperature drops below the 110 degrees F mark to speed up the compost process. If you decide not to monitor the temperature, you can turn the pile every month.

The compost from the bin system is ready when the temperature lowers until it is barely warm and the original materials in the pile are no longer recognizable. It is possible you will have a few pieces that are not quite "finished," which is fine; throw them into the first bin to start the next pile of compost. The compost should also be a rich black-brown color, moist, and have an earthy smell.

How to use compost

Now that you have this great rich soil, it is time to add it to your garden. If you do not want any bits left in your compost, you can run it through a compost sifter, which is wire mesh in a frame, that will leave you with only soil. The bits and pieces that do not go through the sifter can go back into the compost pile. You can do several things with this nutrient rich-soil but treat it as you would any rich fertilizer or potting soil. There are several ways you can use your compost:

• As a mulch to hold water — you can spread it about 3 inches thick on the base of plants, trees, shrubs, or perennials in the garden. If there are some unfinished pieces in your compost, they are fine to use here as they will continue to break down over time.

- To fertilize the garden — you would want to dig the compost into the existing garden, going down several inches or more to work the compost in.

- To make a compost tea — some compost tea is natural byproduct of compost. If there is no liquid in your compost, you can steep a shovel full of compost in a bucket of water for a few days. After a few days have passed, remove the compost material, put it back in the compost pile, and simply water the plants with the compost tea. If you want, you can put the compost into something like an old towel, cheesecloth, or burlap bag before putting it into the bucket of water.

- As a topping for your lawn — often called a lawn dressing, you can add a 1- to 3-inch layer of compost on top of the existing grass. The compost works its way into the ground as the grass grows through it. Because it is a great way to fertilize the grass, adding compost in the spring or fall may eliminate the need to fertilize throughout the rest of the season.

Many people add the compost into their gardens in fall or spring, whenever it is ready, digging it in as they turn their beds over. Whichever way you choose, your plants will benefit from adding compost.

Perfect Combinations

There are also some plants that really work best with each other, which is why they are considered "perfect combinations". Here are some of that you may want to try yourself.

- Cabbage and Tomatoes. Tomatoes are able to repel the Diamondback Moth larvae which are infamous for chewing cabbage leaves and leaving large holes in them.

- Nasturtiums and Cucumbers. Cucumbers make use of Nasturtiums as trellises while Nasturtiums are able to repel the dreaded cucumber beetles. They also serve as natural habitat for ground beetles and spiders which are predatory insects.

- Ragweed/Pigweed and Peppers. Ragweed and Pigweed are good weeds that are able to make the soil fertile and are able to protect plants from being infested by pests.

- Corn and Beans. This combination has been used for thousands of years, as you've read in the beginning of this book, and they are both able to attract beneficial insects such as leaf beetles and leaf horns. Aside from that, they also provide shade and trellis to each other, making sure that they both grow well and become beneficial for humans.

- Dill and Cabbage. They support each other in the sense that dill attracts wasps that eat pests and worms, making sure that the cabbages grow without holes.

- Chives and Roses. Garlic repels the pests that feed on roses, and they also look great when they are planted next to each other.

- Tall Flowers and Lettuce. Tall flowers such as Cleomes and Nicotiana give lettuce shade.

- Sweet Alyssum and Potatoes. Tiny flowers of sweet alyssum attract predatory wasps and also act as shade for the potatoes.

- Catnip and Collard. They reduce beetle damage.

- Spinach and Radishes. They are both able to repel leaf miners and radishes are able to grow safe and well when planted with spinach.

- Dwarf Zinnias and Cauliflower. Dwarf Zinnias are great because their nectar lures predatory insects like ladybugs; and they are known to hunt down and eat common garden pests.

- Melons and Marigold. Marigold repels nematodes just as well as chemical treatments do.

- Love-in-a-mist and Strawberries. They are great for aesthetic purposes.

Here are a couple more companion plants that you can plant in your garden

- Anise. Anise is a good host for predatory wasps which repels aphids and also camouflages the odor of the other plants in order to protect them from pests. Anise is best planted with Coriander or Cilantro.

- Amaranth. Amaranth is an annual plant that grows mostly in tropical conditions and is very beneficial when planted near sweet corn stalks. It acts as shade for the corn which is able to moisten the soil and allow corn to grow better and faster. Amaranth also plays host to ground beetles which are predatory insects who feed on common pests.

- Bay Leaf. Bay leaf repels moths and weevils and can also act as a natural insecticide. Bay leaf is best planted with Tansy, Cayenne Pepper and Peppermint.

- Beets. Beets add minerals to the soil, especially nitrogen that most plants need in order to grow. They are great fertilizers for the soil, too, as they contain 25% magnesium and are best planted with melon and corn.

- Bee Balm. When planted with tomatoes, bee balm is able to improve the growth and flavor of the tomatoes. Bee Balm also attracts bees and butterflies for pollination and is also great for aesthetic purposes as it always looks good and fresh.

- Buckwheat. Buckwheat is a good cover crop as it is full of calcium and is also able to attract beneficial insects such as butterflies and bees, and repels pests such as aphids, flower bugs, pirate bugs and predatory wasps away. Buckwheat can also provide the soil with phosphorous which other plants may also be able to benefit from.

- Chards. Chards are good not only as vegetables but also as ornamental plants that make pollination possible by attracting beneficial insects. They are best planted with tomatoes, roses, beans, onions and cabbages.

- German Chamomile. This is an annual plant that is able to improve the flavor of cucumbers, cabbages and onions and also act as host to wasps and hoverflies. German Chamomile also gives the soil protection by providing it with sulfur, potassium and calcium and also by increasing oil production in the herbs. Because of increased oil production, more people are able to benefit from their plants by making different kinds of aromatherapy oils.

- Clover. Clover works as cover crop or green manure and is best planted near grapevines to attract beneficial insects and make pollination possible. When planted around apple trees, they are able to repel wooly aphids and also reduce cabbage aphids once planted near cabbages. Clover is also able to increase the amount of ground beetles that are great for destroying non-beneficial insects.

- Castor Bean. Castor bean is a poisonous plant that is very effective in repelling moles and mice. And because it is poisonous, you need to be careful where you plant it.

- Chrysanthemums. Fondly called "mums", they are able to repel nematodes which destroy most plants easily. They are also used as botanical pesticides as they are full of Vitamin C that repels most pests, especially Japanese beetles. They work well with daisies in attracting beneficial insects in pollinating your garden.

- Comfrey. An underrated plant, Comfrey is beneficial because it gives calcium and potassium to the soil and also is a good medicinal plant. It also prevents foliage and is a good compost activator as well as nutrient miner. It is best planted with avocadoes.

- Costmary. This flowering plant is very effective in the repulsion and killing of moths.

- Dahlia. While it looks harmless, dahlia is actually able to repel nematodes.

- Four-o-clocks. These flowers are able to poison the dreaded Japanese beetles but you also have to be careful because being around these flowers too much is also toxic to humans.

- Flax. Flax is used in most diets and is full of linseed oil and tannin that are very useful against the Colorado Potato Bug.

- Hemp. Hemp is very useful when planted near brassicas as it is able to repel bugs and pests.

- Hyssop. Hyssop is able to repel cabbage moths and flea beetles and is best planted with grapes and cabbages. Hyssop is also able to attract bees which are good for pollination. More often than not, bees make hyssops their homes, which is good for you as this means that your garden will be pollinated even more.

- Horehound. Horehound belongs to the Mint family and is able to attract beneficial insects such as Icheumonid and Braconoid wasps that consume flies and other insects that feed on your plants.

- Lamium. Many gardeners and farmers think that Lamium is awesome because it is able to repel potato bugs which infest most plants and are definitely not good for anyone's garden.

- Lavender. Lavender provides you with great essential oils and is also able to repel non-beneficial insects such as moths and fleas. It is also able to protect plants from whiteflies. Lavender is best planted during the winter season so it could bloom in spring.

- Larkspur. Larkspur is able to kill Japanese beetles but you have to be careful around it as it is also poisonous to humans.

- Marjoram. Marjoram is able to improve the flavor of most fruits and vegetables and also attracts butterflies and bees so pollination could happen. It's always best to grow sweet marjoram as it gives the best results.

- Morning Glory. Morning Glory attracts hoverflies and also makes the garden more beautiful as it is a vine.

- Stinging Nettles. These plants attract bees and are also full of calcium and silica that are essential for invigorating plants and improving resistance to diseases and also give the soil the nutrients it needs in order for plants to grow healthy and well.

- Okra. While it is not a vegetable favored by many, Okra is very useful as it gives shade to lettuce especially during the summer season and prevent lettuce from wilting. It is also able to protect eggplants and peppers from strong winds. It is also great when planted with peas, cucumber, basil and melons as it also repels aphids away.

- Opal Basil. Opal Basil grows annually and is able to repel hornworms. It is best planted with oregano, petunia, asparagus and peppers and must be kept away from sage and rue.

- Peach. Peach Trees give shade to asparagus, grapes, onions and garlic and may help repel tree borers and most other pests and insects.

- Hot Peppers. Hot peppers protect most plants' roots from being rotten and provide shelter for smaller plants, especially chili peppers and prevent other plants from being dried up or wilted. It is best planted with okra, green peppers and tomatoes.

- Pennyroyal. A great plant that repels fleas, mosquitoes, gnats, flies and ticks.

- Purslane. Is a good cover crop for corn and makes the soil healthy and fertile.

- Rye. Prevents germs from targeting your plants and is great when planted near tomatoes and broccoli as well as with other vegetables.

- Soybeans. Soybeans provide nitrogen for the soil and also repel Japanese beetles and chinch bugs.

- Turnip. Turnip is also able to provide a lot of nitrogen to the soil and is best planted with peas and cabbage. Do not plant near potatoes though as turnip stunts their growth.

- White Geraniums. White Geraniums are effective in repelling Japanese beetles.

How to Get Started

Once you know which plants you want to grow and what your primary goals for companion planting are, it's time to get your system into action.

Cost, Materials, Location and Time

The cost of establishing a new garden can be quite variable, depending on a number of factors. First among them is whether you want to start your garden from seed or buy seedlings that are already somewhat established. Seeds are far less expensive than seedlings, but the advantage of the latter is that you can plant them right away in a prepared bed, instead of starting them indoors and transplanting them.

Assess your budget and how much time you want to commit to getting the garden started, and base your decision on that. To maintain a companion garden, you don't need too many materials. A source of water is of course essential, whether it is a rain barrel, well pump, or spout. Beyond that, a sturdy spade, a garden rake or hoe, and a trowel are all you need to garden with.

These are the gardener's basic tool set, and with them you can maintain any patch of garden easily. While you can buy them new, if you are on a budget you can always look for them at garage sales or thrift shops. Make sure you are getting good quality, however – they will get a lot of use, and you don't want flimsy tools that will wear out easily. Locate your garden in an area that gets a lot of sun through the growing season. You can assess the sunlight simply by checking shadows throughout the day to see which areas get the most light. Very simply, you do not want tall buildings or trees shading the area you will locate your garden in. Additionally, the garden should be in an area that is well-drained.

Do not locate your garden at the bottom of an elevated area that will flood it with rain runoff. And if you can locate it conveniently close to your house, it will make maintenance and harvest a much easier job. The amount of time you spend on your garden is also based on several factors, such as the size of the garden, how many different plants you are growing, and how eager you are to invest a lot of effort in maintaining it.

But the majority of your time will be spent on establishing the garden: one of the major benefits of companion planting is that it saves you a lot of time on a day-to-day basis. Since the plants are providing one another with nutrients, pest control, and weed control, you don't have to spend as much time performing these tasks yourself.

Be prepared to spend a few afternoons establishing your garden, and after you've done so, you won't have to spend more than an hour or two a week on watering, checking for pests and weeds, and monitoring the plants' growth and vitality.

Compost and Soil Maintenance

For starters you will need to prepare a productive, healthy soil. Whether you are adapting a new or unused piece of ground to a companion garden space, it can be tempting to try to finish the preparation phase as quickly as possible and get straight into production. But building soil with the right texture, with a good blend of different sized mineral particles and organic matter, will help ensure your plants have the best foundation to grow well.

Your companion garden will need a rich, healthy soil to be fertile and productive. The amount of time you spend preparing the soil will pay off huge dividends in the long run, so it is certainly worth it. Your crops' vigor and overall health will be greatly affected by how effectively you prepare the soil. The most productive garden soil has 5-10% organic matter: this includes fallen bits of plant and animal detritus, decaying leaves, and humus.

While this amount does not seem particularly large, just a small amount of organic matter can go a long way to ensuring the soil is healthy. Decaying organic matter provides nutrients to the soil and improves its structure, creating a loose, crumbly loam that is easier for roots to move through. It helps small particles of clay bind together into larger pieces, which improves drainage, and it helps to hold water in soil that would normally be dry, sandy, and infertile.

To build up the organic content of your garden bed, add about an inch of compost or well-finished livestock manure every year as an amendment to the soil. You can also add coarse mulch such as four inches of straw or dead leaves. If you have deep, raised beds, you will need to add more organic matter, and the same applies if you are working in a particularly hot climate, in areas that are heavily used, or if you have sandy or heavy soil.

It's also important to make sure the soil is properly aerated. This ensures that microscopic life can flourish, creating the right conditions for organic matter in the soil to be broken down into nutrients the plants can use. In a smaller garden, you can use a spade or spading fork to turn the soil. Loosen the top eight to twelve inches as much as you can, and work compost or manure into it as you do so. Use a hoe or a rake to break up clumps of soil and form a smooth, level surface.

If the soil in your garden is particularly heavy or rich with clay, you may want to consider renting a rotary tiller to break it up. These machines have churning tines that cut through dense soil. While they do not dig as deeply as you can with a spade, the depth they provide will usually be enough, particularly if you plan to establish raised beds. While renting a rotary tiller costs more than turning the soil by hand, you can usually finish the job more quickly with one. If your garden plot is particularly large, it can be well worth the investment.

Creating Gardens in Limited Spaces

In a companion garden, you can organize planting arrangements in many different ways, based on your goals and the amount of space you have. One of the major advantages to companion planting is that it allows you to get more out of smaller spaces because you can mix crops together in ways that maximize the amount of space available.

Double Rows are a simple way to combine two types of crops. This is a great technique for growing bush beans or cucumbers alongside lettuce or other greens. This system allows you to grow a weed-suppressing canopy (or "natural mulch") that reduces the amount of work you have to do. Double rows are also a great way to plant climbing vegetables on either side of a trellis.

Wide Rows can be up to five feet across. This is just wide enough that you can reach the plants in the middle of the row from either side. This allows you to walk around the bed instead of on it, which will help prevent soil compaction. The broad growing area lets you plant several kinds of companion plants in a staggered formation, or side by side across the row.

Wide rows are perfect for growing lots of small plants like leafy greens and root crops in a small area. You can interplant leaf lettuce, carrots, radishes, and onions in staggered rows in the spring. You can also grow larger plants in a wide row, with insect-repellant flowers around the outside.

Local Climate Conditions and What to Grow

Climate conditions can be astonishingly variable from one latitude to the next, and because of that it's vital that you find out what hardiness zone you live in. Hardiness zones are geographically defined climate regions that have similar growing conditions throughout. They're generally arrayed along fairly well defined latitudes, but can be subject to the effects of geographical features such as mountains, large bodies of water, and local climate conditions.

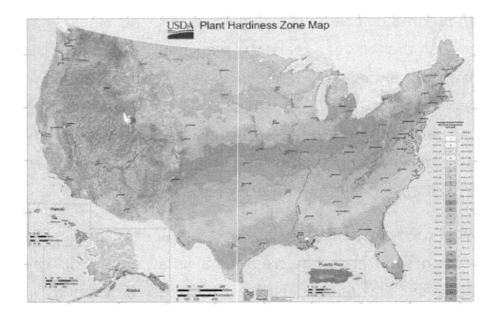

USDA Plant Hardiness Zone Map

All regions of the world have hardiness zone maps available that will tell you what is best to grow there as well as when local frost dates generally occur. Familiarize yourself with these frost dates as well as what plants are best suited to grow in your region's hardiness zone.

Different Methods

There are a few different companion planting methods that have been shown to work particularly well. You may have already heard of some of them. The three sisters' technique, square foot gardening, container gardening, and the seven layer system known as the forest garden are some of the most popular.

The Three Sisters

This is a companion planting technique that was developed by Native Americans to enhance the growth conditions of some of their staple crops: corn, beans, and squash. This technique uses the companion methods of structural support and nutrient cycling. Three or four bean plants are planted around the base of each corn plant in rows, with squash planted between the rows. The beans fix nitrogen in the soil for the corn plants, which in turn provide structural support for the bean vines. The squash also benefits from the nutrient cycling of the beans, and its broad leaves provide natural mulch to shade out weed plants.

Square Foot Gardening

Square Food Gardening is a companion technique designed to increase the amount of yield from a small garden space. In this method, long rows are abandoned in favor of a grid system. The grid is composed of 1′ x 1′ squares, and each square is dedicated to a different crop. This method allows the gardener to intercrop numerous cultivars in the same location more easily. This is useful because, with a square foot garden, you can incorporate companion plants, pest repelling flowers, attractive plants to lure pollinators and predatory insects, and cycle nutrients. This allows you to get the most effective companion planting system in the smallest space.

Container Gardening

This is a useful method for making the most of small spaces, as well as gardening when you only have a balcony, rooftop or patio available to work with. You can apply any of the principles of companion planting to your container garden for pest control, nutrient cycling, and structural support just as you would if you were planting in the ground. An additional aspect of companion planting in containers is the fact that you have more spatial variability to work with. You can trail creeping vines from the edges of containers, especially if they are hanging baskets. And you can build successively taller layers in the container, working from the outside edge inwards.

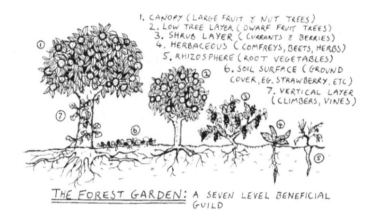

1. CANOPY (LARGE FRUIT & NUT TREES)
2. LOW TREE LAYER (DWARF FRUIT TREES)
3. SHRUB LAYER (CURRANTS & BERRIES)
4. HERBACEOUS (COMFREYS, BEETS, HERBS)
5. RHIZOSPHERE (ROOT VEGETABLES)
6. SOIL SURFACE (GROUND COVER, EG. STRAWBERRY, ETC)
7. VERTICAL LAYER (CLIMBERS, VINES)

THE FOREST GARDEN: A SEVEN LEVEL BENEFICIAL GUILD

The Seven Layer System

This is an intensive companion planting method in which the garden is structurally modeled after the composition of a forest. Forests have complex understories with multiple ecological levels. In a seven layer garden, tall fruit trees make up the upper canopy layer. The next layer is composed of smaller nut trees or dwarf fruit trees. Below this is a shrub layer with berry bushes, followed by a layer of medium sized vegetables. The lower layers include root and tuber vegetables and a ground cover of edible plants that propagate horizontally. The final layer is made up of climbing vines that grow up through the other layers.

Companion Planting for Pest Control

Of all the benefits that companion planting can provide your garden, controlling pests is probably one of the most important ones. While companion planting can't eradicate garden pests altogether, it can help reduce the damage caused by them significantly. Effectively companion planting to control for pests starts with observing your garden, doing some simple research, and planning ahead.

Begin by looking for obvious signs of pests in your garden. Are certain plants doing poorly? Are there visible pests or signs of disease? If there are holes in the leaves, you could be dealing with beetles, slugs, or caterpillars. If there are tunnels in the stems, borers are the most likely culprit. If plants are wilting or growing poorly, there are probably aphids, thrips, or leaf hoppers present. Check under the leaves and along the stems, since this is where many pests like to hide and lay their eggs.

Once you know what kind of pests you are dealing with, you should learn everything you can about it. Find out about its life cycle, when it typically appears in the garden, and whether it attacks just certain plants or a wide range of them. Once you have this information, you will be ready to start combining plants to protect against the attackers.

How Plants Deter Pests

Plants discourage pests with a number of different strategies. Some kinds of plants only use one method; others use a combination of properties to fight pests. You can use all of the following methods in your garden to make pests unwelcome.

Making detection difficult is a great way to throw pests off the trail of your vegetables. Many pests are attracted by the smell of certain plants. The cucumber beetle, for example, is attracted to cucumbers by cucurbitacin, a bitter compound. Other pests find their targets using visual cues like color. Because of this, you can fool pests by planting off color cultivars of their favorite vegetable.

Red cabbage, purple cauliflower, and purple kohlrabi are less attractive to cabbage loopers. Yellow berries attract fewer birds than red berries do. Japanese beetles are less attracted to dark-colored flowers. Some plants are less attractive to pests because of their structure or location. Aphids prefer the shade, so they'll pass by exposed pea vines in favor of densely branched plants.

Repelling attacks is the next line of defense. Once pests find a target plant, they have to break through its natural defenses, such as tough, hairy, or waxy leaves that make penetration harder. Hairy-leaved tomatoes, for example, deter many chewing insects. Other kinds of physical defenses can help reduce pest damage. Corn ears with long, tight husks are less prone to damage by earworms or birds. Beans and peas that have tough, leathery pods can resist injury by weevils.

Tomatoes and Marigolds

Companions as Repellents

Take advantage of the natural ways plants can repel pests in your companion garden. You can mask the scent of certain crops with more pungent species, use plants and their extracts to deter or kill pests, and create physical barriers to keep flying, predatory insects from flying away from your garden.

Powerfully scented plants produce various chemical compounds that can discourage most pests. Bold citrus or perfumed fragrances given off by the volatile essential oils in mint, thyme, lemon balm, and lemon geranium often drive pests away. Many herbs produce these compounds, making them natural choices as companion plants.

Mixing these strong-smelling plants among crops that are prone to pest attacks can help mask the scent of target vegetables and keep them safe. Garlic is another very strong-smelling plant with a well-deserved reputation as an excellent companion plant. It is often recommended for interplanting with roses or tomatoes to keep pests away. Garlic also has fungicidal and bactericidal properties that can protect tomatoes from blight.

Decoy and Trap Crops

Growing plants that you know pests will be attracted to might sound crazy, but it's a great way to use companion plants to your advantage. The trick is to plant a few cultivars that pests will find more attractive than your good crops. The pests will be more likely to damage the decoy plants than your crops. Trap cropping does take some advance planning and careful observation.

Your trap crops must already be growing when insects are out in force. If the pest problem only occurs at a single time of year, a single planting of trap crops can be enough to control them. But if a pest tends to be active through the growing season, you will need to plant a succession of trap crops. For example, you can sow nasturtiums among your tomatoes and roses every two weeks throughout the summer.

As soon as you find aphids swarming on one crop of nasturtiums, destroy the plants and the pests quickly so the aphids don't have a chance to reproduce. Keep trap crops like nasturtiums as close as you can to the target crops. Watch them carefully, and be ready to kill the pests before they breed or move on to other targets.

Companion Vegetables

This offers you an in-depth look at how to plant various vegetables and the best and worst companion plants to go with them. Remember that most vegetables like a nutrient-rich soil full of well-rotted compost and mulches. Even if the individual plant instructions do not mention this fact, make sure your garden bed is richly prepared before beginning. There are a few vegetables that do well in sandy beds, like carrots, but most do better in well dug over dirt that has been enriched with nutrients in preparation for the long growing season. All beds will also benefit from additional nutrients throughout the growing season.

The following are guidelines you can follow, but take the time to make this fun. Mix up the planting and interplant carrots with beets and radishes or try planting kohlrabi with both to take advantage of the nutrients at the surface level versus deeper root levels. Vegetable gardening can be a fun and rewarding experience.

Asparagus

Asparagus prefers to grow in the same spot year after year, so pick a full-sun location for best results or partial shade in a spot where it will not need to be disturbed. You will need to purchase asparagus crowns from your local garden center or nursery catalog. The crown will have a strong root system but the top growth will be dormant. Plant the crowns in early spring for most locations; if you live in a warmer climate, you can plant in late winter. The asparagus will need to be planted deep so make a trench approximately 6 to 7 inches deep. Spread the bottom of the trench with wood ashes or bone meal and compost if you have it. There will be instructions on the asparagus when you purchase it, so make sure you read and follow them.

In general, soaking the roots first, preferably in a compost tea, is a good start. Then lay them on their side in the trench approximately 1 foot apart. Make sure the rows are 3 to 4 feet apart. You will the fill in the trench slowly as the sprouts appear but only cover the stalks and be sure to leave the foliage uncovered. With time, the trench will fill in and the asparagus foliage will now be above ground level. It is important to be diligent with the weeding and you should aim to lay down mulch once the trench is filled in.

Asparagus has many companion plants, including the family of aster flowers, dill, coriander, basil, comfrey, and marigolds, which will deter beetles. Parsley appears to increase the growth of both plants when they are grown together. Tomatoes and asparagus help each other; tomatoes protect against asparagus beetles and a chemical in the asparagus juice deters nematodes from tomato plants. There are no known bad companions for asparagus; however these plants do better when they are not close to onion, garlic, or potatoes.

Beans

There are different types of beans available, like snap, dry, and bush. Some will have different companions, both good and bad. There are some basics that apply to all types of beans. Plant in a full-sun location or partial shade if you live in hot climates. Sow seeds only after danger of frost has past. For scarlet runner beans, which are climbers, supply support of some kind. Thin the seedlings to 5 or 6 inches apart, but leave slightly more space for pole beans.

All beans have the ability to enrich the soil with nitrogen. They all do well when planted with carrots, cauliflower, peas, radishes, potatoes, strawberries, the brassica family, chard, and corn, and they are of great benefit to cucumbers and cabbage. Summer savory is another good companion to beans as it improves the beans' growth and flavor and deters the bean beetles. Marigolds, rosemary, and nasturtiums also deter bean beetles.

Bad companions for beans include garlic, onion, and shallots as they appear to stunt the plants' growth. They are not happy planted close to gladiolas. Beans are prone to diseases, but crop rotation will prevent most of them. There are also companions specific to individual types of beans.

Bush beans

Bush beans, a shrub variety of the snap bean, do well with celery if planted at the ratio of one celery plant to six bush beans. Bush beans do well close to celery and leeks but only if there are only one or two bean plants there. If more than this are planted, then none of them do well. Bush beans will give and receive benefits when planted with strawberries and cucumbers. Bush beans are a bad companion to fennel and onions.

Pole beans

Pole beans, a climbing variety of bean like scarlet runner beans, do particularly well with corn, summer savory, and radish. They do not particularly like beets. They make bad companions with onion, beets, cabbage, eggplant, kohlrabi, and sunflowers.

Broad beans

Broad beans, also called fava beans or horse beans, produce large, flat pods with large beans inside. They are excellent companions for corn, potato, cucumbers, strawberry, celery, and summer savory. They are bad companions with onions.

Beets

Beets are an easy-to-grow crop that prefers a full-sun location and well-tilled soil with good drainage. They germinate well and will need to be thinned to 4 inches apart with rows at least 2 feet apart. Beets are great for the garden as they add in minerals to the soil.

Beets are good companions for lettuce, onions, kohlrabi, and the brassica family. Mint, garlic (which improves the beet's flavor), and catnip help beets grow. If you do not want to plant mints around the beets, you can use mint foliage as mulch. Beets are bad companions to pole beans and gives mixed results next to bush beans.

Broccoli

Broccoli grows best in full sun or partial shade in a well-drained soil. In terms of minimizing disease, plant broccoli where no other brassicas (including cabbage, Brussels sprouts, kohlrabi, and cauliflower) have been planted in the last two years as per crop rotation rules.

Broccoli is a large plant and can reach 3 feet in height so the seeds or nursery seedlings should be planted 18 inches apart after danger of frost has passed. If they do not form heads (broccoli florets) properly, they are deficient in lime, phosphorus, or potash. You can purchase these nutrients at your garden center and add them to your broccoli plants.

Broccoli, like all the brassicas, does well with aromatic plants including dill, which improves the plant's growth and health. Broccoli is a good companion to beets, celery, chard, cucumber, lettuce, onion, potato, and spinach. Flea beetles like broccoli so plant Chinese Daikon and Snow Belle radishes to attract flea beetles away from the broccoli.

Do not plant close to tomatoes, strawberries, pole beans, peppers, or mustards as they are bad companions.

Cabbage

Cabbage needs to spend at least half the time in the shade. You can grow from seed or purchase the plant from a nursery to get a jump on the season. Insects like young cabbages so consider covering the plants with a light-weight cloth when they are first growing. They love compost, fertilizer, and water. If the cabbage's florets do not form properly, the plant is deficient in lime, phosphorus, or potash and you should purchase some from your local garden supply store to add to your beds.

Cabbage, like all the brassica family, does well with aromatic plants including dill, while sage, peppermint, and rosemary help repel cabbage flies. Celery and dill improve cabbage's health and growth. Clover will reduce native cabbage aphids and cabbage worm. Other good companions include onions, potatoes, hyssop, thyme, and southernwood. Wormwood repels white cabbage butterfly. Tansy deters cabbage worm and cutworm, and thyme deters cabbage worm. Nasturtium deters bugs, beetles, and aphids from cabbage.

Bad companions for cabbage are strawberries, tomatoes, peppers, lettuce, eggplants, rue, grapes, and pole beans.

Carrots

Carrots prefer full sun and need a very loose, preferably sandy soil for the roots to grow easily downward. If your soil is high in lime, humus, and potash, you will have sweeter tasting carrots. Low nitrogen levels in soil will decrease the flavor of your carrots. Sow seeds directly into the garden several weeks ahead of the last frost (in warm climates you can sow in fall, winter, and spring).

Sow seeds around ½ inch deep and thin to 3 to 4 inches apart. Thin early before the roots entwine and be careful to not damage the remaining plants.

Plant onions, leeks, rosemary, and sage to deter the carrot fly. Other good companions include lettuce, onions, chives, beans (which are a good source of nitrogen and can help increase your carrots' flavor), peas, peppers, radish, and tomatoes. Tomatoes can stunt the carrot's growth but they will have a great flavor. Bad companions for the carrot are dill and parsnip. If you want to use carrots to attract insects, they need to be able to flower, so plant a few carrots with the intention of leaving them in the ground instead of harvesting them for eating.

Cauliflower

Cauliflower likes a full-sun location in a well-drained soil. Purchase nursery stock to get a jump on the season or sow outdoors after danger of frost has past. Sow in small clusters of several seeds but once they have sprouted, keep only the strongest cauliflower plants. Keep the plants moist when they are young.

For growing instructions and companions, see cabbage as most members of the brassica family have similar growing requirements.

Celery

Celery needs to have a lot of sunshine but can have partial sun for half of the day. Celery requires a rich, moist soil. It is easiest to work with plants from the nursery that you can transplant into the garden when there is no danger of a frost. Plant 8 to 10 inches apart and be generous with compost and water over the growing season.

Good companion plants for celery include beans, leeks, onions, spinach, tomato, and the brassica family. Garlic and chives help keep aphids away from celery. If bush beans and celery grow together, they will strengthen each other. Friends to celery include cosmos, daisies, and snapdragons. Bad companions for celery are corn, lettuce, and aster flowers.

Chard

Chard is an easy-to-grow vegetable. It prefers full sunlight unless you live in a hot climate where they prefer partial shade. Well-drained soil with compost helps chard produce well. For most climates, sow the seeds in the spring and thin to 8 inches apart when the seedlings are about 6 inches high. You can either eat these seedlings or transport them to another spot in the garden.

Good companions for chard include beans, brassica family members, and onions. There are no known bad companions.

Corn

Corn likes full sun and a rich, well-draining soil covered in mulch. Sow several seeds in a hill approximately 1 inch deep and 6 inches apart. When seedlings are close to 4 inches tall, thin them to 1 foot apart. Corn needs a steady supply of water and mulch.

Corn helps beans when grown together (as in the Three Sisters example) and sunflowers, legumes, peanuts, squash, cucumbers, melons, amaranth, white geranium, lamb's quarters, morning glory, parsley, and potatoes all help corn. Marigolds help to deter the Japanese beetle away from corn. Planting radishes around corn and letting them go to seed deters an insect called a corn borer, which is known to be a pest for several agricultural crops. Bad companions for corn are tomato and celery. Pigweed is said to raise nutrients from the deeper earth level to a place where the corn can reach them.

Cucumber

Cucumbers like full sun and can also do well with afternoon shade. Seeds are sown several inches deep a couple of weeks after danger of frost has passed and once the soil has warmed slightly. Plant the bush varieties approximately 1½ feet apart and the vine varieties 2 to 3 feet apart.

Cucumbers have many good companions including corn, beans, sunflowers, peas, beets, and carrots. Radishes can deter cucumber beetles. Keeping dill close to cucumbers attracts beneficial predators and cucumbers attract ground beetles. Nasturtiums improve the cucumbers' growth and flavor. Bad companions for cucumbers include tomatoes and sage.

Eggplant

Eggplant loves heat, so plant it where it can have full sun. It is easiest to purchase started plants then transplant them when there is no longer any danger of frost. It is preferable to wait a week or two after frost has passed to allow the soil to warm up. There are dwarf and standard varieties of eggplant. Plant the standard versions approximately 1½ to 2 feet apart and the dwarf varieties can be 1 to 1½ feet apart. Tie the taller varieties to stakes to keep the fruit from touching the ground.

Good companions for the eggplant include amaranth, peas, spinach, and marigolds, which deter nematodes. Eggplant helps beans and peppers. They are good to plant with corn as they deter raccoons from eating the corn and the corn protects the eggplant from a virus that causes wilt. Bad companions for eggplants are pole beans, fennel, and potatoes. There are mixed results when planted with aromatic herbs.

Horseradish

This is an easy plant to grow and will take over your garden in no time. Find a corner away from most of the plants and consider planting horseradish in containers. It is easiest to purchase a small plant from the nursery and it will grow in most conditions. Plant 1 foot apart and bury the top of the root 4 inches below the surface. Make sure you water this plant well.

If you grow this plant in a container, you can move the containers around. Keep 1 plant in the potato patch to deter the blister beetle and help deter Colorado potato beetle. Horseradish also improves the potatoes' resistance to disease. If you are going to plant it in the potato patch, be sure to dig it up and remove it in the fall to prevent the plant from spreading.

Kohlrabi

Kohlrabi is a cooler weather vegetable that can be planted for both spring and fall crops. Plant in full sun and in well-drained soil. Sow seeds outside four weeks before the last frost. Plant the seeds ½ inch deep and 3 inches apart but thin them to 6 inches when the seedlings are several inches high, which will not take very long as these plants are very fast growing.

Kohlrabi is a good companion with cucumbers, beets, onions, and chives and appears to help protect members of the mustard family. It is a bad companion to strawberries, tomatoes, peppers, and pole beans.

Leeks

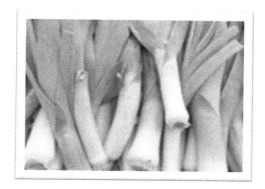

Leeks like a full-sun location that offers well-drained soil. It is easiest to buy leek plants to transplant into the garden around the time of the last frost. Place the seedlings approximately 6 inches apart. Set the plants closer together if you are planting long, thin-stemmed varieties or set them wider apart for thick-stemmed varieties. (Always check the package for specific planting instructions.) Make a hole and set the seedling down so that only an inch of the top of the plant is exposed. Fill it in loosely with soil.

Leeks will improve the growth for celery, onions, and apple trees. Carrots help leeks by repelling carrot flies. Bad companions for leeks are legumes including beans and peas.

Lettuce

Lettuce does best with a mixture of sun and shade. It does not like extreme heat and will need shade during the hottest months or else it will go to seed. Sow the seeds outdoors once the ground has thoroughly thawed and can be worked. If you purchased plants, set them approximately 1 foot apart (this may vary based on the variety so read the label) and sow several times for a lettuce supply all summer.

Lettuce does well when close to radish, onions, kohlrabi, beans (both bush and pole), cucumbers, carrots, strawberries, beets, and sunflowers. Chives and garlic are great deterrents of aphids so plant them close to lettuce. Mints like hyssop and sage repel slugs so plant these plants close to your lettuce if slugs are a problem in your area. Lettuce is a bad companion to celery, cabbage, and parsley.

Onions

Onions are another plant where it helps to purchase plants at a nursery instead of starting the plant from seeds. You can transplant onions into your garden up to two months before the last frost is expected. Any earlier than this and it could be too cold for them. They like a partial to sunny spot and appreciate compost. Make sure the soil is dug over well to allow for good bulb development and weed constantly in the early growth stage as the weeds can crowd out the young onion plants. As the bulbs grow, make sure to keep them covered if they start to push out of the ground.

Good companions for the onion include all the brassicas, beets, lettuce, tomatoes, summer savory, leeks, kohlrabi, dill, lettuce, and tomatoes. Plant onions in the strawberry patch to help the strawberries stay healthy and fight off disease. Pigweed has the ability to raise the nutrients from subsoil and makes them available to the onions. Bad companions for onions are peas, beans, and parsley.

Beginner Mistakes to Avoid

Just like heating up your interest in other things, you could also be burning with excitement over companion gardening. However, it is not always fruitful to be overly thrilled about something as you might oversee important details or perhaps rush things when you have to let time take its toll. This is true for companion gardening as well. Heating up the pot definitely helps but will not be able to sustain it unless you try to control the temperature.

Starting Too Big

One of the most common mistakes that you should never attempt to do is to start big with companion gardening. Even if you have a big lawn or backyard intended for this purpose, you should always try a smaller plot first.

Consider your first plot as an experimental plot. When you have a smaller plot, you can manage it well and also observe if the plants that you have paired really work. After all, since your intention is to produce crops for personal use, then it could be best to have plots that you can readily manage rather than have several plots that you can't actually carefully attend to. It's a bad picture if you have plants dying in front of you.

Not Preparing Your Soil

No matter how good the pair of plants that you intend to put into your garden, your labor will never bear much fruit if you have a poor soil. Soil is the key to growing good produce, as plants typically are dependent on it for most of the nutrients necessary for plant growth, development, and propagation. Before starting your companion garden, it is best that you prepare the soil.

First, the removal of weeds, rocks, and other unwanted debris is important as it may interfere with the optimal growth of your plants. Weeds may compete, not only for space, but also for available minerals in the soil that may hinder or retard your crop's growth. It is also helpful if you study the profile of the soil in your garden so you can estimate also how much water will be necessary.

Clayish soils are gummy-like in appearance and when you hold it, the lumps are very visible. Such soil does not promote good air and water circulation and is not healthy for companion gardening.

Sandy soils, characterized by too many grains and breaking easily, also are not advisable for companion gardening as it allows water to drain easily. This may leave your plants wilting as water provided to them may not actually be absorbed readily by the roots as the grains of the sand are too fine to hold water molecules in place. Apart from draining water easily, sandy soils often have low nutrient concentration and are also unlikely to promote healthy crops.

Regardless of whether the soil in your garden is clayish or sandy, you can improve it by mixing compost into it. Decayed organic matter typically makes up the compost added to soils. It is a good source of nutrients for plants and at the same time improves the quality and texture of the soil. You can readily produce your own compost by allowing leaves, peels, and other biodegradable items to degrade.

Composting is done simply by creating a layer of biodegradable items then covering it with soil. This is performed alternatively, then the compost pit is watered regularly to hasten degradation. Compost may also alter the pH of the soil and so it is important that you also measure this factor. Most plants grow optimally in neutral soil (pH 7) and others like camellias and rhododendrons prefer soil of acidic pH. Lilacs and clematis also favor a more basic soil., keeping this in mind helps to augment your success in companion gardening.

Establishing Plots in Shady Areas

Another thing to avoid in companion gardening is to position your garden in the shady section of the lawn or the backyard. Though other gardeners think of their own convenience first when establishing their home plots, this is be very beneficial in terms of achieving your goal of producing good quality crops or flowers. This is because sunlight is an important ingredient in a plant's physiological functions. The food-producing mechanism of plants can only be possible when sunlight is present. Though the requirements of plants for sunlight appear to vary, over-shading has never been known to help in crop production. Choose a site that is relatively exposed to the sun at the peak of the day.

Excessive Watering

It's good to water your plants once established in the plots, but it is never fruitful to have garden plants watered excessively. Too much water may actually soak the roots and endanger it (as it may actually promote root rot) or it may actually destroy sensitive parts like buds and new leaves promoting early abscission. Fungal diseases like lights and powdery mildew are also associated with overwatering.

It is best to study the water requirements of the plants that you plant in your companion garden. For reference as to whether there's a need to water your garden or not, you can stick your finger on the soil (up to the second knuckle) and if the soil is dry, you may water the plants. However if it is still wet, there is no need to add water to the soil. You should also avoid watering the plants from above.

If possible water it below the stem so that it ensures faster root absorption of available water and prevent wastage. Control the pressure when you water your garden. Too much pressure may not only break off some parts of the plants but will also promote soil erosion and root exposure.

Conclusion

Thank you for making it to the end of **Companion Planting**, with this book as a guide, you can enjoy the benefits of companion planting to make your garden healthier and more productive, and without having to work as hard to repel pests or keep your crops robust. Starting with a solid foundation of healthy soil that is rich in organic matter, carefully plan out how to arrange your companion garden to get the most out of your space.

Companion planting is receiving a lot of attention from the scientific community because it can help reduce the need for harmful chemicals in farming. Home gardeners are re-discovering this information and using it to their benefit.

Remember that increasing yield is not just about spatial efficiency, but also about extending the growing season to be as long as possible. By applying the principles of companion planting, you can have a beautiful, productive garden that takes care of itself. Companion planting is an important way to shift to using more sustainable, organic methods of keeping your garden healthy.

The key to successful companion planting is properly planning where the plants in your garden are going to go. You've got to carefully consider how each of the plants in your garden are going to interact with one another and then place them in the best possible locations to take advantage of those interactions. The biggest limitation in regard to companion planting is the knowledge of the gardener. Arm yourself with as much knowledge as possible before you ever put on your gardening gloves.

Keep in mind that one of the most common mistakes that you should never attempt to do is to start big with companion gardening. Even if you have a big lawn or backyard intended for this purpose, you should always try a smaller plot first.

Assess your budget and how much time you want to commit to getting the garden started, and base your decision on that. To maintain a companion garden, you don't need too many materials. A source of water is of course essential, whether it is a rain barrel, well pump, or spout. Beyond that, a sturdy spade, a garden rake or hoe, and a trowel are all you need to garden with.

Remember that in Companion planting, there are literally millions of types of insect, but not all of them are pests determined to devour your crops. There are a lot of species which are referred to under the umbrella term of 'beneficial insects' which provide a natural form of pest control. For many gardeners, including myself, they are an essential part of organic and natural gardening.

Once you know which plants you want to grow and what your primary goals for companion planting are, it's time to get your system into action. This book will explain how to get started with companion planting in the real world – taking your plans and making them a reality in your garden.

By weaning your garden off of chemical fertilizers and insecticides, and using natural methods to keep your plants healthy and free of pests, you will be improving not only your plants' health but your own as well. You'll also be improving the environmental and carbon footprints. And your garden will be more robust as a result and better equipped to handle variable weather conditions, droughts, and disease. Good luck!

CPSIA information can be obtained
at www.ICGtesting.com
Printed in the USA
BVHW040301121120
592962BV00012BA/1102